Disabilities / Different Abilities

A New Perspective for Job Hunters

by Paula Reuben Vieillet, MA

Employment Options, Inc.
St. Petersburg, Florida

ACKNOWLEDGEMENTS

I am grateful to all those people who have contributed through their instruction, encouragement, edits and for believing in my abilities. I would also like to thank my numerous clients, without whose questioning and searching for a more meaningful and productive life, this work would not exist.

I especially want to thank Cathy Reuben for her willingness to share her legal perspective and resources and Victor Vieillet, Sarah Vieillet and Gerald Hall for their support and feedback.

Many thanks and hugs to Nancy Greenfield for her editting , encouragement and continuous belief in this manual.

I would like to thank my family, for being there, always.

Published by:
Employment Options, Inc.
P.O. Box 46694
St. Petersburg, Florida 33741
(800) 441-3114
www.myemploymentoptions.com

ISBN -13:#978-097152220-6

About the Manual

This is a hands-on workbook which will help the job hunter who has a disability or different abilities secure employment. Step by step, this manual guides the job hunter through the vocational process in an honest and positive manner so as to get results.

It is designed for individual usage or in conjunction with a trained professional.

The first section, **Getting to Know You,** addresses self-esteem, personal values and job goal definition and includes motivational strategy.

The second section, **Facing Workplace Discrimination,** reviews application and interviewing functions with a focus on eliminating discrimination in the hiring process. Typical concerns of job hunters are answered in a straightforward and informative manner.

The third section, **Ready, Set, Go** deals with feelings and concerns regarding re-turning to work and includes a handy reference guide of available resources for job hunters with disabilities.

A note to all job hunters from the author:

If you are reading this manual, either on your own, or as part of a rehabilitation plan, it is because you have suffered or are likely to face difficulties in getting hired due to discrimination. Although the Americans with Disabilities Act of 1990, enforced by the Equal Employment Opportunity Commission, was created to protect you, the fact remains that discrimination is very real. Discrimination laws take many years and individual efforts before the discrimination laws are truly integrated.

Just a word to let you know how important it is to stand up for your rights as a person with many different abilities and assets:

Throughout history, different populations have had to fight for their right to live equally and to have equal opportunity. Slowly, through individual and group efforts, people are becoming freer to live without fear, practice their religions, vote, travel, and work without imposed barriers due to race, sex, nationality, sexual preference, age or physical and mental abilities.

As a society, it is essential that we learn to respect each other's differences and live peacefully. All individuals, have something valuable to share. Much of the progress in our workplaces has been achieved because of an individual's need for accommodations. These include flexible work schedules, computer programs that respond to vocal dictation rather than typing and ergonomic workstations. These accommodations have improved the quality of life for many people, not only people with disabilities.

As humans we all have our strengths and weaknesses. Some people are very skilled with their hands, others are gifted with words; some are athletic, others are intellectual. As individuals, it is important that we develop our strengths and not allow our weaknesses to rule our lives. Sometimes it feels as though our only strength has been taken away; however, no matter how real that feels, there is still something special about you that can be developed and shared. Your most important contribution may be in your future.

In this manual, I challenge you to focus on your strengths, to understand, accept, and accommodate your weaknesses, and to learn techniques to make this journey a little easier and more fruitful. No matter what your condition, I urge you to stand up for your right to equality, the right to be human, the right to dignity, and the right to equal access to employment.

Best wishes,

Paula

CONTENTS

Getting to Know You . . .

Getting to know you. . .

This section will help you through the initial process of identifying workplace preferences and values. It will be easy to answer some of the items and others may require a little thought or may not have a clear-cut response.
This is o.k.

Each one of us has individual preferences and strengths. The more self-awareness we possess, the better we are able to communicate this information in a job interview.

This section is intended to encourage you to gain self-awareness.

In addition to completing these exercises, it is helpful to consult with a vocational counselor who has experience with standardized testing and who also has knowledge of the current job market, to measure your current aptitudes, assess transferable skills, and to help you in identifying appropriate job goals.

What interests you ?
(Check all that apply)

- ❑ Mechanics
- ❑ Science
- ❑ Investigating
- ❑ Helping People
- ❑ Technology
- ❑ Sales
- ❑ Managing People
- ❑ Clerical Tasks
- ❑ Mathematics
- ❑ Reading
- ❑ Writing
- ❑ Sketching
- ❑ Decorating
- ❑ Cooking
- ❑ Sports
- ❑ Movies
- ❑ Fashion
- ❑ Indoor Activities
- ❑ Driving
- ❑ Building Things
- ❑ Gardening
- ❑ Home Maintenance
- ❑ Music
- ❑ Shopping
- ❑ Animals
- ❑ Religious Activities
- ❑ Traveling
- ❑ Fine Dining
- ❑ Theater
- ❑ Working Out
- ❑ Children
- ❑ Senior Citizens
- ❑ Parties
- ❑ Outdoor Activities
- ❑ ________________
- ❑ ________________

What is your ideal work environment?
(Check your preferences)

- ❑ Small company
- ❑ Large organization
- ❑ Inside work
- ❑ Outside work
- ❑ Job with traveling
- ❑ Stationary position
- ❑ Routine work
- ❑ Varied work duties
- ❑ Frequent interaction with people
- ❑ Little interaction with people
- ❑ Wear business clothes
- ❑ Wear jeans
- ❑ Wear a uniform
- ❑ First shift
- ❑ Second Shift
- ❑ Third Shift
- ❑ Week-ends

What do I really need from my job?

(Pick 4 items from the following words and list in order of importance)

- **High salary**
- **Flexible schedule**
- **Stable employment**
- **Meaningful work**
- **Great co-workers**
- **Challenging work**
- **Learn new skills**
- **Convenient working hours**
- **Non-stressful work**
- **Benefits**
- **Room for growth**
- **Advancement with company**
- **Immediate employment**
- **Other**

Use words from either column

Current Goals	Five Year Goals
1.	1.
2.	2.
3	3.
4.	4.

Knowing your strengths!

(Choose 7 words from the following list which best describe you)

- Alert
- Capable
- Courteous
- Competent
- Dependable
- Effective
- Empathetic
- Good listener
- Hard-working
- Imaginative
- Independent
- Orderly
- Outgoing
- Persistent
- Patient
- Attentive
- Common sense
- Cooperative
- Consistent
- Detail-oriented
- Efficient
- Enthusiastic
- Innovative
- Loyal
- Genuine
- Motivated
- Objective
- Professional
- Poised
- Responsible
- Committed
- Confident
- Creative
- Cultured
- Diplomatic
- Energetic
- Fast learner
- Honest
- Cheerful
- Punctual
- Mature
- Organized
- Productive
- Perceptive
- Sincere

My Strengths
1.
2.
3.
4.
5.
6.
7.

What makes you the person for the job?

(Fill in the blanks using your six strength words from the previous page)

---

1. An employer would benefit from hiring me because I am .... and I can perform this type of work well.

2. You can count on me because I am ....

3. Employers appreciate my ability to be ....

4. I have always been .... in my work.

5. My co-workers appreciate the fact that I am ....

6. In my previous job, I was very .... which was just what my employer needed.

7. I think it would be in your best interest to hire me because I am .... and this is a very important quality in this job.

Body Language

Body language is a good indication of how one feels and is often a better communicator than speech in expressing attitudes.

By consciously adjusting our body posture, a change in how others' perceive us is inevitable. Subconsciously, our own attitudes will change as we try to portray a more positive body posture.

Cooperative: Relaxed body, no furrows on forehead, friendly greeting, open stance

Lack of Confidence: Head down, slumped posture, slow pace, difficulty sustaining eye contact

Enthusiastic/Confident: Puts weight on balls of feet, sits towards the end of the chair, posture erect, chin up, tilted head, relaxed forehead

Hostile/Defensive: Arms crossed, intense and glaring eyes, hands clenched, tight facial features

Impatient: Taps foot, shifts positions frequently, looks away, fidgets with hands

Lying: Does not make good eye contact, looks away when speaking to you, puts hands in front of mouth

Control: Tight lips, leans forward, closer than normal comfort zone, hands on thighs

Frustration: Short breathing, restless hands, pushes air through nose, tense body posture, eyes squinting

A Menu of Jobs

Find the right career which is physically suitable. There are many jobs which do not require heavy physical exertion or where reasonable accommodations are common. This list includes some light and sedentary positions to consider depending on your interests and abilities. Some are entry-level and others require formal education. This list is not exclusive and job duties may differ depending on the company. A good reference source for career exploration is the Guide For Occupational Exploration published by the U..S. Department of Labor, which is available in most libraries.*

Manufacturing

- Assembly
- Soldering
- Microscopic assembly
- Quality control
- Engineer
- Tool design

Clerical

- Word processor
- Data entry
- Secretary
- Bookkeeper
- Receptionist
- Customer service

Sales and Management

- Sales representative
- Sales clerk
- Marketing
- Real estate agent
- Insurance agent
- Business manager
- Consultant
- Financial planner

Hospitality

- Hostess
- Cashier
- Hotel manager
- Events coordinator
- Front desk
- Reservationist
- Travel agent

Technology

- Computer programmer
- Technical support
- Electronic repair
- Robotics
- Purchasing

Artistic

- Actor
- Writer
- Graphic artist
- Musician
- Agent
- Artist
- Jeweler
- Web site designer

*See Glossary

A Menu of Jobs

Professional

- Rehabilitation counselor
- Attorney
- Teacher
- Minister
- Social worker
- Accountant
- Architect
- Scientist
- Human resources

Medical

- Admissions
- Quality assurance
- Respiratory therapist
- Ward clerk
- Medical lab tech
- Dental lab tech
- Dietician
- Speech pathologist
- Ultrasound tech
- Home health-sitter
- Patient care coordinator
- Audiologist
- Medical Coder

Paraprofessional

- Paralegal
- Teacher's aide
- Drafting
- Environmental technician

Miscellaneous

- Mortgage clerk
- Title clerk
- Loan officer
- Telemarketer
- Seamstress
- Motorcycle mechanic
- Boat mechanic
- Electric tool repair
- Driver
- Inspectors
- Purchasing
- Locksmith
- Security officer
- Construction superintendent
- Insurance adjuster
- Neon tube bender
- Cosmetologist

Identifying job goals

What are your preliminary job goals?
(Sample: Delivery driver)

1.

2.

3.

What would you like to find out about this job?
(Sample: What are you delivering?)

1.

2.

3.

What are your major concerns regarding your ability to do this type of work?
(Sample: Is the merchandise heavy?)

1.

2.

3.

What questions would you like to ask an employer?
(Sample: What kind of merchandise do you deliver?)

1.

2.

3.

Facing the job market

Facing the job market. . .

All of your questions regarding your rights under the Equal Opportunity Employment Act as a job hunter with a disability will be answered as you complete this section.

Reasonable accommodations are discussed in depth, and you will have a much better understanding how to accommodate your particular disability in the workplace.

Common forms of discrimination are noted. You will learn how to best present yourself so as to allow prospective employers to learn all about you: strengths as well as weaknesses - an honest, yet non-discriminatory approach.

Your strengths will be recognized...It is nice to be needed.

Facing workplace discrimination?

It is illegal for employers to discriminate in hiring people because of race, color, gender, national origin, religion, age or disability.

Civil rights protection is provided by the

Equal Employment Opportunity Commission.

These are some of the ***illegal questions*** you may be asked which may be used to ***discriminate*** against hiring you.

- ***What is your race?***
- ***What is your age?***
- ***Are you married?***
- ***What is your religious background?***
- ***Do you have any children?***
- ***Do you have a back injury?***
- ***Have you ever been on Workers' Compensation?***

Facing workplace discrimination?

These are some more of the ***illegal questions*** you may be asked which may be used to ***discriminate*** against hiring you.

- ***Are you disabled?***
- ***Do you take any medications?***
- ***How many sick days did you take last year?***
- ***Do you have any health problems?***
- ***How long have you been handicapped?***
- ***Why are you in a wheelchair?***

Employers may **not** ask you questions about your disability, only your abilities.

You may be asked to voluntarily disclose your disability for affirmative action purposes.

This is intended as a guide. Contact the EEOC for specific questions concerning the laws and your rights.

How to protect yourself against discrimination

Address the concern, not the question!

Some of the typical concerns or stereotypes :

Older workers :

* May be frequently ill
* Too old to learn new information
* Slow
* Not too many work years remaining
* Only wanting to work part-time
* Too much time needed to train

Address the concerns:

If age is the concern, sample responses may include:

- **I am not sure how old you need to work in this job, but I am hoping to work for my next company for 10 years.**
- **I am sure my excellent work experience and years of dependability will be an asset to your company.**
- **I am open to learning new information.**
- **I am a good listener.**

Some of the typical concerns or stereotypes :

Persons with disabilities :

* Too difficult or costly to accommodate
* Will drive up health insurance costs
* May re-injure themselves
* Will increase workload on co-worker
* Frequently absent
* Dangerous to themselves or others

Address the concerns:

If disability is the concern, sample responses may include:

- **I had a great attendance record at my past job.**
- **I am able to perform all of the functions of this job.**
- **I might need a little help with ___________ .**

  Would that be a problem?
- **I can do everything in the job description, except for unloading the trucks. Is there a way that we can work around this?**

Some of the typical concerns or stereotypes :

Family status:

Single Persons
*Not stable
*Job hopping

Single persons with children
*Will miss work because of children's illnesses, activities
*Children come before work

Married
*Unwilling to travel
*Unwilling to work long hours

Sample responses:

- **I am hoping to grow with a company.**
- **I love this area.**
- **I have excellent work references.**
- **I had 20 sick days to my credit when I left my last job.**
- **I am willing to do what it takes to get the job done.**

What if they ask me...?

Do you have a back injury ?

This question is **NOT** permissible under the Americans with Disability Act. Address the concern, not the question.

Sample responses :

- What do you do in this job that concerns you?
- I should not have any trouble working in this position.
- Is this a very physical job?

Are you on Workers' Compensation ?

This question is **NOT** permissible under the Americans with Disability Act. Address the concern, not the question.

Sample responses :

- I am currently looking for work.
- What exactly do you do in this job that this concerns you?

Do you have any children ?

This question is **NOT** permissible under the federal anti-discrimination law.

Sample responses :

- Is this a prerequisite for this job?
- I have a very dependable work history and I am free to travel, if that is your concern.

What is your age ?

This question is **NOT** permissible under the federal anti-discrimination law. Address the concern, not the question.

Sample responses :

- I am looking for a long-term employment, if that is your concern.
- I am a fast learner and still open to new information.

What if they find out that I am on Workers' Compensation? Will I be terminated? Will I be covered by health insurance?

The law prohibits discrimination, and your Worker's Compensation status has no relevance to your ability to do the job. Your medical coverage through the employer will be the same as any other employee who starts work.

Can employers require a medical exam?

Yes, ***after*** a conditional offer of employment has been made.

Any examination must be job related and necessary for business. It must be given to all conditional hires and results must be stored in a file separate from your personnel file.

What if they find out I have a medical condition?

As long as your medical condition does not interfere with your ability to perform the essential functions of the job, it cannot by law affect the hiring decision.

If you have a **qualified disability**, employers are required to make a reasonable effort to accommodate your disability.

Can employers ask you about your current medical condition or status of your Workers' Compensation injury?

No, any inquiry in regards to physical condition is not allowed under the guidelines of the American with Disabilities Act, unless the question specifically **relates** to the **essential functions** of the job.

Can you lift 50 pounds?_________ Yes? ________ No?

This question is allowed, **if the essential functions of the job require the lifting of 50 pounds.** For example, a delivery driver who regularly delivers large packages may be asked that question.

If you are applying for a clerical position, in which **normally there is little lifting,** then this question would **not** be appropriate as the **lifting of 50 pounds is not essential** to the job for which you are applying.

The law requires that employers only consider a person's work qualifications and abilities to perform the essential job functions of the job, and specifically states that employers may not ask about disabilities until after a conditional job offer, so as to encourage hiring persons with disabilities.

What can employers ask?

It is very common for employers to ask on the application

the following question :

"Are you able to perform the essential duties of the job with or without reasonable accommodations?"

(If you are unable to answer YES to this question, Job goals should be revised, or reasonable accommodations reviewed.)

▶ Can you demonstrate or tell me how you would perform the job?

If the employer has **reason to believe** that the applicant will need reasonable accommodations due to an obvious disability (person is in a wheelchair, blind, etc.) or because the applicant has **voluntarily disclosed** that he has a disability, then this question is permissible. Ask to see the job description so you know exactly what are the essential job functions.

What can employers ask?

- **Can you meet the employer's attendance requirements?**

  Employers are allowed to ask about your ability to be at work, as it is not disability related, and as there are many reasons why a person is unable to be at work.

- **Have you ever been arrested or convicted?**

  This question is permissible.

- **Do you currently use illegal drugs?**

  This question is permissible, the current use of drugs is **not** protected under the ADA.

When is the best time to talk about your disability?

Unless there is a need for reasonable accommodations, it is **not** necessary to talk about your disability at all.

If reasonable accommodations are indicated:

From a legal standpoint: After there is a conditional job offer, a person should inform the employer that he has a disability so that accommodations can be put in place.

From a practical standpoint: As a general rule, do not voluntarily disclose information about your disability before you have had a chance to focus on your abilities and not before a job offer unless it will increase your chances of securing employment.

What does it mean by reasonable accommodations?

A reasonable accommodation is a modification at the workplace which can be accomplished without posing undue hardship on the employer to allow a person with a qualified disability

Some types of reasonable accommodations may include :

- **Assistance with occasional lifting of heavy objects.**
- **A stool or ergonomic chair.**
- **Flexible work hours.**
- **A change in break schedule.**
- **An ergonomic keyboard.**
- **Modified non-essential duties.**
- **A job coach.**

Research shows that most accommodations cost less than $200 !

How do I know if I will need accommodations?

Ask questions to find out what duties are essential to the job:

- Is there a lot of lifting required on the job?
- What are the job duties? Let them tell you what the job is all about.
- What kind of person do you hope to hire?
- What exactly would I be doing?
- Is there a lot of standing? Is there a stool? Could I bring in a stool?

Quantify :

- Would I be typing all day ?
- How often would I be lifting batteries ?
- Would you say I would be climbing ladders every day or once a week ?
- How often does the merchandise come in ?

If it sounds like you can do most of the work, then it may be appropriate to suggest reasonable accommodations.

How to suggest reasonable accommodations

- Do you think it would be okay if I arranged my time a little differently? Could I do some typing for an hour and then some filing?
- Is there anyone who can help me if I need to get a battery?
- It is difficult for me to climb ladders. Would you be able to schedule someone else on the jobs that require climbing a ladder?
- Would you be able to schedule my day off on Wednesdays when the truck comes in? I have difficulty physically carrying more than 25 pounds and it sounds like this day would involve a lot of lifting.
- It sounds like I have exactly the qualifications you are looking for to fill the position, but it would be easier for me if I could work flexible hours. Would that be possible?
- I would love to work here, but I am unable to stand all day. Would it be possible to use a stool?
- If there are accommodations which are possible but a little inconvenient, try to assist the employer by demonstrating how you would be able to function at the job.

Sometimes, employers will not be able to accommodate you.

For example, a stool may present a safety hazard, or the company is small and they do not have anybody who can help. It is not always reasonable for employers to modify jobs.

Thank them, ask for a referral, and keep looking!

▶ What if I get the job and find out that there is more lifting or typing involved than disclosed in the interview ?

You are covered under the Americans with Disabilities Act, whether you are working or not.

If you find that you need help with accommodations, either prior to your becoming employed or when you are working, you can call a toll-free national hotline :

Jobs Accommodations (JAN) 1-800-526-7234

Internet address : http://janweb.icdi.wvu.edu.

This is a free consulting service which provides information on available aids, devices and methods for accommodating workers with disabilities.

Other resources include :

Naric - **N**ational **R**ehabilitation **I**nformation **C**enter
8455 Colesville Rd.
Silver Spring, MD 20910

1-800-346-2742

Internet address : www.naric.com/naric

This organization has an extensive web site providing information related to disability, including a library of current and prospective research projects, funding for rehabilitation projects and a database of over 60,000 publications of literature on disability.

President's Committee on Employment of People with Disabilities

Internet address : www50.pcepd.gov/pcepd/ztextver/joblinks.htm

This site includes links to employers who have indicated interest in recruiting and hiring qualified individuals with disabilities.

Assistance for persons with disabilities

- **State Vocational Rehabilitation:**

  This agency work sdirectly with people with disabilities and illnesses that interfere with the person's ability to work and may be able to help with obtaining appropriate medical treatment, vocational retraining and job placement assistance. Each state has own protocols.

- **Division of Workers Compensation:**
  Each state has its own rules and regulations. Services are targeted to assist and to educate persons who have had injuries on-the-job in regards to their rights and options.

- **US Department of Veterans:**
  Provides medical and rehabilitation services for qualified veterans nationwide at medical centers, and veterans affairs offices.

- **Non-Profit Agencies:**
  Some of the agencies which serve persons with disabilities nationwide include: Goodwill Industries, Association of Retarded Citizens, Epilepsy Services, Lighthouses for the Blind, Deaf Services, United Cerebral Palsy, United Way, and American Association of Retired Persons.

Where to Report Discrimination:

The Equal Employment Employment Commission has fair practice centers nationwide to register complaints and encourage compliance.

Call 1-800-669-3362 for written information

or

visit them on the Web at: **http://www.eeoc.gov**

Your personal accommodations

List accommodations which most probably you will need.
(examples: stool, ergonomic keyboard or chair, change in break schedule, help with lifting heavy objects)

Where or how can they be obtained?
(examples: Be specific - what store or catalog sells what you need?)

How much do they cost?

Who will provide these accommodations? Who do I need to ask?
(Example: Prospective employer, rehabilitation agency, insurance company, self)

From a legal standpoint: Employer pays for accommodations (except for personal items like glasses, wheelchair, hearing aid, etc.).

From a practical standpoint: Other resources may be considered.

NOTES:

On Your Mark, Set, GO!

On your mark! Set! Go. . .

Review and practice of this section will help you to master the application, interview and follow-up process.

It is helpful to complete the practice application and contact your references, letting them know you are in the process of job hunting. It also helps to run through a mock interview using your customized sample responses with someone else asking you sample questions. This will solidify the learning process.

Be sure to follow-up after you have applied with a company. It reminds the employer that you are interested in the job.

As you start working, remember that the employer was willing and able to make reasonable accommodations. It is okay if there are some things that you are unable to do. Get help if you need. You are worth it. You have a lot to offer.

TELEPHONE TECHNIQUES

Hi, my name is _______________, I am calling to see if you are doing any hiring for a________________? (use name of a specific job)

If yes, ask the following :

- **What are you looking for?**

Listen carefully and ask appropriate questions like:

- **Is the job very physical?**
- **Is there a lot of walking?**
- **Is there a lot of lifting?**

Or whatever concerns you may have with this particular type of job.

If the job sounds okay say:

- I am very interested in this position.
- I have experience as a __________________ and I am looking for this kind of position.

Ask questions to determine the primary duties of the job.

Specifically ask questions relating to work conditions.

TIPS ON COMPLETING APPLICATION FOR EMPLOYMENT

Many people have difficulty determining what to write for **reason for leaving** on the job application.

Be honest, but positive. If you write that you have been fired, lost job due to an injury or that you left for medical reasons, it gives a negative impression.

Use positive terms

Suggestions:

- Lay-off
- Career change
- More suitable position
- More money
- Better job
- Relocation
- Reorganization

It is **not lying** when presenting yourself more positively.

If you were a carpenter and injured your elbow and it is painful for you to use a hammer, **a better job would be any job that did not provoke pain on a regular basis**.

Because you want to be honest, you will be tempted to write on your application everything about yourself, please do not.

Remember it is illegal for employers to ask you about illnesses or disability. If you tell all, you may not get a chance to try returning to work.

It is human nature to discriminate

For Example:

You have two friends who both want to borrow your new car.

- One of the friends had been in an automobile accident—it was not his fault, but he was hurt and the car needed a lot of repairs.
- The other friend had a clean driving record.

To whom would you lend the car?

Generally speaking, a person would be less likely to lend the car to someone who had an accident. This could be called discrimination—since it was not the other friend's fault and was just bad luck. Nonetheless, concerns do arise when insurance and property are involved.
This is very similar to how employer's choose prospective employees and although it may not seem fair, the information will affect how a personnel director makes their employment choices.

The ADA is designed to limit discrimination by making it illegal to ask disability related questions to applicants.

If you volunteer information that is illegal for the employers to ask, then it provides information to the employers which will be considered in the hiring decision and may influence the employer **not** to hire you.

By focusing on your qualifications, and not disclosing unnecessary details about your injury or condition, the prospective employer will be **less likely** to have concerns that will go against hiring you.

I am having trouble remembering my exact dates of employment.

This is common– Tips for remembering.

Can you remember how old you were when you started working there or finished employment?

Was it fall, winter, spring or summer?

If you have children, was it before or after they were born?

Was is before or after you were married?

What kind of car were you driving to work?

Where did you live when you worked there?

If memory fails you, I would suggest you call your previous employer to get exact dates of employment. If the business is closed, then use your best estimate.

How do I address the problem of gaps in employment on a job application?

- On an application, it is difficult to address gaps in employment. This is best handled in an interview or on a resume.
- Many people have gaps in their work history. Time off to care for children, ill parents, or return to school is not unusual. Also, it does take time to find the right job. Sometimes it takes a little time to assess the right direction.

▸ I have a criminal record. Should I mention this on the application?

Disclosure of criminal records differs in each state. Most of the states require that if you have been convicted of a felony and if the application includes this question, that you disclose this information. States have different regulations as to whether or not a juvenile felony would need to appear on an application and other regulations regarding expunging of criminal records and misdemeanors.

Certain types of positions may not be appropriate in light of your criminal history.

If you have been convicted of theft, then it may not be appropriate to apply for a locksmith position.

With a history of multiple DUI's then a driving career may be out of the question.

A history of drug abuse would probably preclude you from working in a pharmacy and would need to be disclosed if applying for a nursing or physician position.

▸ The job I would like to work in requires bonding. Can I get bonded if I have a criminal background?

Any 'at risk' person including ex-offenders, ex-addicts, welfare recipient, persons with poor credit, youth lacking a work history, individuals dishonorably discharged from the military and any other person unable to secure employment without bonding are eligible for bonding through the Federal Bonding Program.

To locate the approved Federal Bonding office nearest you:
Call 1-877-872-5627. This national jobs and training referral service can also direct you to local agencies for other employment related services.

Checking References

There are two types of references.

- ☑ Work References
- ☑ Personal References

A **work reference** involves calling or writing the employers whom you have listed under **work history.**

Example:

FORMER EMPLOYERS (LIST BELOW LAST FOUR EMPLOYERS, STARTING WITH LAST ONE FIRST

DATE/MONTH/YEAR	NAME & ADDRESS OF EMPLOYER	SALARY	REASON FOR LEAVING

Personal References

Personal references are those listed in the reference section of an application.

Example:

REFERENCES
GIVE BELOW THE NAMES OF THREE PERSONS NOT RELATED TO YOU, WHOM YOU HAVE KNOWN AT LEAST ONE YEAR

NAME	ADDRESS	TEL.NO.	BUSINESS	YEARS KNOWN
1.				
2.				
3.				

A **personal reference** is a person that you have chosen to vouch for your integrity, work performance, ability to get along with others, honesty, values, dependability, character, and any other concerns that the employer may have regarding your employability with their company.

A personal reference is generally one of the following::

- Personal friends
- Clergy
- Neighbors
- Previous co-workers
- Supervisor

I do not have many friends. May I list relatives?

Most companies do not accept references from relatives. It is acceptable to list people who live in another city which may be relevant if you have recently moved.

Personal References

A prospective employer may ask your personal references any questions without restrictions.

Prep your references

- ☑ Ask them if they would mind being a reference.
- ☑ Let them know what type of job you are pursuing.
- ☑ Update them on your medical progress and why this would be a good job for you.

This will help your personal references get a clearer picture of your abilities and give them a chance to think about what they would say.

Your references may be also be able to provide you with valuable feedback as well as moral support.

You never know,
your reference may have knowledge
of a job opening that would be just perfect for you.

Work References

Concerns about what a previous employer will say during a reference check is one of many job hunters' greatest fears.

In order to avoid possible charges of libel or discrimination under the American with Disabilities Act, many prior employers chose to only disclose to a prospective employer:

Dates of Employment

Whether or not the person is eligible for rehire.

Regardless of Possible Legal Complications:

Some employers will disclose more than what is recommended, especially if it is a smaller company.

Be sure **<u>not</u> to list this employer as a personal reference** if you are afraid of a bad reference.

It may be worthwhile to have a friend or counselor call or write your references and try to check them as if they are a prospective employer.

This way you will have a better idea of how your previous employer may handle a reference check.

Work References

Sometimes the employer will provide a poor reference outside of recommended legal guidelines. Unless you are willing to invest time and money into a legal battle another option to consider is to:

Choose a specific person on your application as the reference contact.

- Someone with whom you have had a favorable work relationship.
- Pick a person who knows your work and who is able to give the prospective employer a favorable impression.
- Pick a person with whom you had a good rapport and knows your work.

Suitable work references:

- A Supervisor
- Human Resource Director
- Co-worker

Call the people whom you would like to list as a work references.

Let them know your current status:

Update them about changes that may have occurred in your health, outlook, or circumstances. Let them know what type of work you are pursuing. This will prepare the person if they are called for a reference check.

Be sure to **thank them for their assistance.**

Work References

Obtaining a clearer picture of what your references will say may alleviate some of the anxiety that often accompanies a termination of employment.

What if my chosen person is not willing to provide a reference—referring me back to human resources?

Many companies have a policy that prohibits managers or co-workers from giving out work references.

This policy is usually implemented because the company is afraid of people in the company disclosing information which is in conflict with legal guidelines that limit what a previous employer can say to a prospective employer, thereby exposing the company to a possible lawsuit.

TO DO LIST

☑ Obtain a **written letter of personal reference** from a supervisor or co-worker and attach it to the job application or resume. (not on company letterhead)

☑ Bring to the interview **copies of positive job evaluations** or other documentation from previous employers which supports your work abilities and work ethics.

☑ Make a **portfolio of your work** for the prospective employers' review.

☑ Get a **letter of reference** from someone from another company or customer whom you serviced as part of your employment.

Work References

Another option is to send a written reference request to your previous employer. Enclose an envelope which is stamped and addressed for their convenience.

Sample letter:

July 30, 2001

To Whom It May Concern:

We are considering (your name, social security number) for employment and are checking her references. Thank you very much for your assistance.

Did (your name) work for your company? If so please note the dates of employment.

Is Ms./Mr. (last name) eligible for rehire? If not, why not.

Comments?

Sincerely,

Joe Trimball,
President

I, authorize the release of this information to (person who is checking references for you).

____

Signature Date

What if I Get a Bad Reference?

If the reason that the employer stated you would be ineligible to be rehired is due to an injury or illness, it is not necessary or recommended to disclose details about your physical condition or reason for termination in the interview.

Why did you leave your last job? Sample interview responses:

- I am looking for a position which is more intellectually challenging.
- The type of job I worked in was very heavy. I would be better suited to a job which is not as strenuous.
- I am looking to work in a position that does not require frequent or constant ________________(standing, climbing, bending, typing, lifting, etc.).
- The position no longer fit my needs.
- It was a mutual agreement. I was having difficulty with the physical aspects of the job.
- I went back to school so that I could work in a different and more suitable field.
- I took some time off to re-evaluate/explore my career goals. It seems like your company may be a good match for me.

APPLICATION FOR EMPLOYMENT

PRE-EMPLOYMENT QUESTIONNAIRE
EQUAL OPPORTUNITY EMPLOYER

PERSONAL INFORMATION

Date ______________________

NAME (LAST NAME FIRST) SOCIAL SECURITY NO.

PRESENT ADDRESS CITY STATE ZIP CODE

PREVIOUS ADDRESS CITY STATE ZIP CODE

PHONE NO. ( )

EMPLOYMENT DESIRED

POSITION DATE YOU CAN START SALARY DESIRED

ARE YOU EMPLOYED ——— YES ———NO

IF SO, MAY WE INQUIRE OF YOUR PRESENT EMPLOYER ——YES ——NO

EVER APPLIED TO THIS COMPANY BEFORE? ——— YES ——— NO

WHERE? WHEN?

NAME AND LOCATION OF SCHOOL	YEARS ATTENDED	SUBJECTS
HIGH SCHOOL		
COLLEGE		
TRADE OR BUSINESS		

SUBJECTS OF SPECIAL STUDY/RESEARCH

CERTIFICATIONS

US MILITARY **RANK**

FORMER EMPLOYERS (LIST BELOW LAST FOUR EMPLOYERS, STARTING WITH LAST ONE FIRST

DATE/MONTH/YEAR	NAME & ADDRESS OF EMPLOYER	SALARY	REASON FOR LEAVING

SPECIAL QUALIFICATIONS

ARE YOU AUTHORIZED TO WORK IN THE UNITED STATES ———YES———-NO
(NOTE If you are hired, you wil be required to submit proof of legal right to work in the United States)

CAN YOU PERFORM THE JOB WITH OR WITHOUT REASONABLE ACCOMMODATIONS?

_______YES _______NO

HAVE YOU EVER BEEN CONVICTED OF A FELONY? _________YES ________NO
(NOTE: If yes, please explain)

REFERENCES
GIVE BELOW THE NAMES OF THREE PERSONS NOT RELATED TO YOU, WHOM YOU HAVE KNOWN AT LEAST ONE YEAR

NAME	ADDRESS	TEL.NO.	BUSINESS	YEARS KNOWN
1.				
2.				
3.				

AGREEMENT: *(Please read following statements carefully).*

I certify that all information on this application and any other material provided by me is true and complete. I agree that falsified information on this application shall be grounds for dismissal.

I authorize this Company or its agent to investigate and/or verify all information in this application, including contacting all person, school, current employer (if applicable), previous employers and other individuals or entities named herin (and those named on accompayning resume, if any). I hereby authorize my former employers and other third parties named on this application to release information pertaining to my work record, habits and performances. In doing so, I hereby release them and the Company and its agents from all liability which may flow from the release of such information.

I also understand and agree that no representative of the company has any authority to enter into any agreement for employment for any specified period of time, or to make any agreement contrary to the foregoing, unless it is in writing and signed by an authorized company representative.

DATE____________________SIGNATURE ____________________________________

INTERVIEWED BY_____________________________DATE______________________

Resumes

▶ Do I need a resume?

The primary purpose of a resume is to obtain an interview.

If you are able to find employers interested in interviewing you without a resume, then you may not need a resume.

▶ How is a resume different from an application?

A resume is like a picture of yourself. It presents an image of your skills, abilities, interests, and experience.

A resume can highlight skills or interests that you would like to use more in your next position.

An application asks for specific information. Generally an application asks for previous employment history, education, and references. An application leaves little room to talk about your interests, goals, or transferable skills.

If you are changing careers, it is helpful to have a resume so you can emphasize those skills and abilities which would be used in another occupation.

▸ What is a transferable skill?**

A transferable skill is a technical term that describes activities that you have performed in your past jobs that will also be used in a new job.

▸ How do I know if my resume is any good?

Resumes are a bit like taste buds.
You may like a resume and the person next to you may think it needs revising.
A Good Resume Gets Results!!

A Good Resume Gets Results!

The average **human resource director** will spend about **twenty seconds reading a resume**. In that case, a one page resume summing up your work experience and skills is preferable.

If your work history is quite involved and you are applying for a higher level position such as CEO, a longer resume or curriculum vitae may be more appropriate.

If you are applying for a job that requests a scannable resume that means that your resume will be read by a computer which will be looking to identify buzz words or words specific to your profession such as CPA or MCP.

How do I know if I need a scannable resume?

Usually the employer will indicate that they are looking for a scannable resume. Guidelines for scannable resumes are a little different.

- Use of italics, underlining, shadows, bullets and boxes are difficult for the computer to read and are not recommended.
- Use of common fonts such as Times Roman and Courier is recommended.
- Avoid use of two column formats and graphics.

▸ I am not sure how to get started on a resume.

It may help you to look at different resume books to choose the style you like best.*

▸ Should I go to a professional resume writer to write my resume?

It can be helpful to hire a professional resume writer or work with a vocational or career counselor.

Pick someone who is familiar with the job market and who can objectively describe your skills and help you in developing an objective.

You can also look at the sample resumes and build your own.

A functional resume which works well for persons changing careers

Bill Thompson
9100 Main Street.
St. Petersburg, Florida 33712
(727) 956-0199

OBJECTIVE: *Technical- electrical and Customer Service*

PROFILE: Well rounded, courteous, creative, and flexible individual

SUMMARY OF QUALIFICATIONS:

- Hands on experience with AC/DC circuiting, hydraulics, pneumatics, magnetics
- Experience with step up and step down transformers and familiar with Y+ and Delta
- Electrical wiring up to box - including 240 x 480 volt electric and 3 phase electric and controls
- A/C experience with thermostats, refrigeration, controls, and solenoids
- Computer literate - Windows - Typing - 30 wpm
- Team player - good at interpersonal skills

EDUCATION:

St. Petersburg Tech Institue, St. Petersburg, Florida 3.0 GPA
Certified as Industrial Electrician
VICA member - Vocational Industrial Clubs of America
Air Conditioning and Heating
Accomplishments: Rotary scholarship recipient
Public Works Academy, St. Petersburg, Florida

WORK HISTORY:

1999 - 1999 **Minute Press.,** St. Petersburg, Florida
Machine Press Operator
- Assembly line work collecting and stacking phone books

1998 - 1999 **Hideaway Grill,** St. Petersburg, Florida
- Cook - worked way up from prep to grill cook

1997 - 1998 **Town and Country Yacht Club,** St. Petersburg, Florida
Maintenance/Housekeeping
- Maintained facilities - setting up and breaking down banquets

1990 - 1995 **Suncoast Dome,** St. Petersburg, Florida
Commissary Manager
- Working supervisor of seven people
- Responsible for scheduling, distribution, manifesting, stocking, janitorial and maintenance

RELEVANT WORK EXPERIENCE:

American Utilities - Electrician helper

HOBBIES:

Surfing the Internet and cooking

Bill Thompson had been working in a heavy job as a press operator and needed to get into something lighter.

His education and skills were listed first since they were his strongest selling points.

His objective stressed his customer service and technical background with the hopes that he would be considered for a position in customer service, as a industrial electrician or light maintenance worker.

Always put your strongest points first!

Why did you leave out dates of education?

Putting in dates of education tips an employer off as to the age of the applicant.

Also since Bill had some gaps in employment recent history, putting his education first took the focus off the gap.

The advantage of a resume is that it can help present an applicant's positive qualities so that the prospective employer is interested in interviewing him.

He was offered two positions with this resume.

- The first offer was as a telephonic customer service representative for a major telephone company.
- The second was as an assistant maintenance supervisor.

Mary Lincoln needed to change careers because she had carpal tunnel and would no longer be able to cut hair all day. We were very specific with her job goal and stressed her accomplishments.

MARY LINCOLN

2052 Marietta Road
St Petersburg, Florida 33713
(727) 321-0273

OBJECTIVE: Cosmetology Instructor

PROFILE: Professional, Stable, Self-motivated, and Productive individual

SUMMARY OF QUALIFICATIONS:

- Licensed cosmetologist
- Certified in Joe Blasco make-up
- Seasoned manager
- Excellent interpersonal skills

WORK HISTORY:

1995 - 2000 Fashion Haircuts - St. Petersburg, Florida
Salon Manager

- Supervised up to 10 person staff - scheduling, hiring and firing
- Organized and led monthly meeting

Accomplishments: Sixth Highest in Sales in Nation
Won Color Competition

1993 - 1995 Sandy Morris Glamour Studio, St. Petersburg, Florida
Make up artist- Stylist

1990 - 1993 Fantastic Sams, St. Petersburg, Florida
Hair stylist

1986 - 1988 Ready Dispatch, St. Petersburg, Florida
Field Representative

- Evaluated and trained drivers

PROFESSIONAL LICENSES: **Cosmetology -** Manhattan Beauty School, Tampa, Florida
Refresher courses in Cosmetology
CPR & First Aid -Manatee Community College, Venice, FL

COMMUNITY INVOLVEMENT: **Broadway Productions**, St. Petersburg, FL - Make-up and casting

HOBBIES: Movies, cooking, and computers

(References available upon request)

Getting started on your resume.

NAME
address
City, State, Zip
Telephone e-mail:

OBJECTIVE:

PROFILE:

SUMMARY OF QUALIFICATIONS:

-
-
-
-

WORK HISTORY:

19__ - 20__

____

-
-

Accomplishments:

19__ - 19__

____

-
-

19__ - 19__

____

-
-

EDUCATION:

MILITARY

PROFESSIONAL LICENSES:

COMMUNITY INVOLVEMENT:

HOBBIES:

(References available upon request)

Getting started on your resume.

OBJECTIVE: Use the job goal that you listed in the first chapter of the manual *Getting to Know You*

Example:

OBJECTIVE: Construction Supervisor

If you are unsure as to exactly what type of job you are looking for then use a more general objective ...

To create a more general objective use words from section *What do I need from my job*?

What is your ideal work environment?

- ☑ Challenging work
- ☑ Room for growth
- ☑ Large company

Example:

OBJECTIVE: A Challenging position in large company with potential for growth.

PROFILE: Use your answers from *Getting to Know You*

- ☑ Competent
- ☑ Dependable
- ☑ Persistent
- ☑ Energetic
- ☑ Diplomatic

Or from

What Interests You?

- ☑ Mathematics
- ☑ Helping people
- ☑ Managing people

Example:

PROFILE: A competent and dependable worker who is good with numbers and enjoys working with people.

Or

Example:

PROFILE: An energetic, diplomatic and persistent professional with 15 years experience in the construction industry.

A profile creates an image so that the prospective employer to begins to know you.

SUMMARY OF QUALIFICATIONS: Use your transferable skills and any other skill which you may have acquired through hobbies, taking care of your family or in a class.

Example:

In your previous job as a carpenter you measured and cut wood and metal products, used tools including hammers, saws, nails, and screws.

Skills

Ability to read blueprints
Lay out a floor plan
Supervise workers
Purchase materials
Estimate costs
Knowledge of building codes and inspection procedures.
Ability to utilize hand tools
Ability to measure accurately.
Closing sales

Try to quantify your skills:

Include:

How Much?

How Many?

What kind?

Where?

Example:

OBJECTIVE: Construction Sales and Estimating

PROFILE: An energetic, diplomatic and persistent professional with 15 years experience in the construction industry.

SUMMARY OF QUALIFICATIONS:

- Knowledge of material and labor costs for framing, trim and flooring
- Estimating experience in new and remodels up to $250,000
- Able to read blueprints and lay out a floor plan
- Knowledge of building codes and inspection procedures
- Ability to measure accurately
- Excellent at closing sales and customer service

Or

OBJECTIVE: Construction Supervisor

PROFILE: A competent and dependable worker who is good with numbers and enjoys working with people.

SUMMARY OF QUALIFICATIONS:

- Supervised crews of up 10 workers
- Purchased materials for job sites
- Able to manage multiple job sites simultaneously
- Estimate labor costs for projects up to $250,000
- Knowledge of building codes and inspection procedures
- Familiar with local vendors, distributors, carpenters and laborers
- Customer friendly

Use information from your application

Example:

WORK HISTORY:

19__ - 20__

____

-
-
-

Accomplishments:

19__ - 19__

____

-
-
-

19__ - 19__

____

-
-

or

____

If you have a long work history or have a lot of gaps -just list related work history without the dates.

Example:

RELATED WORK HISTORY:

Ten Years experience working with ABC Tools in purchasing

Five Years experience at Buy Rite Furniture as a sales clerk

▸ Do I need a cover letter?

Not if it keeps your from sending out your resume.

A cover letter can take different forms:

- ➡ A fax sheet
- ➡ A standard cover letter
- ➡ A personal cover letter that addresses a specific person and identifies the job for which you are applying
- ➡ A detailed cover letter that describes your particular circumstances and talks about why you would like to work at this company

Unless a cover letter includes information vital to the job duties or information that can not easily be portrayed on a resume, a cover letter serves little purpose except to address the resume to a specific person. It is better **NOT** to send a detailed cover letter as it often takes a lot of time to write and it is easy to make writing errors.

Some prospective employers request a cover letter. In those cases be sure to include a cover letter. For higher level positions a cover letter may be helpful as it can help the interviewers get to know you as well as provide a sample of your writing ability.

➡ TIP: If you are faxing resumes to multiple companies on the same day, write the contact information on the fax sheet in pencil. You can erase the names and numbers and keep the rest of the information. This goes quite quickly and gets your resume in front of more people.

Fax Cover Letter

Bill Thompson
9100 Main Street.
St. Petersburg, Florida 33712
(727) 956-0199

To:	Brad Leffers c/o Inway Industries	**From:**	Bill Thompson
Fax:	(813) 931 –1212	**Date:**	
Phone:	(813) 931-1265	**Pages:**	2
Re:	Customer service	**CC:**	

☐ **Urgent** ☐ **For Review** ☐ **Please Comment** ☐ **Please Reply**

Comments:

Dear Mr. Leffers,

Thanks for taking a look. Feel free to call me with any questions.

Sincerely,

Bill Thompson

Sample Cover Letter

John Tanner
8119 W. Willow Ave.
Chicago, Ill. 98894
E-mail: jtann@aol.com

Jane Willow c/o
Mane Corporation
2222 Main Street
Chicago, Ill. 98339

Date

Dear Ms. Willow,

I am interested in exploring management positions with your construction company. In my last position I managed a crew of ten and was responsible for managing labor costs, ordering materials, and budgeting.

As I am finding that carpentry only uses some of my abilities, I am looking for a management opportunity which will challenge me.

Thank you so much for your consideration. I would love the opportunity to help your company increase productivity and profits.

Sincerely,

John Tanner

Did they receive your resume?

Follow-up is essential!!

When you follow-up with a prospective employer, your resume is automatically placed on the top of their stack.

Sample follow-up call

Hi, could I speak to (insert name of contact person).
(if they are unavailable, ask the person answering the phone if they know if your resume was received)

I am just checking to make sure that you received my resume.
(The primary purpose of this call is primarily to see if they did receive resume and to get it on the top of the stack*)*

Did you have any questions?
If they are not too busy—ask them "**When do you expect to be interviewing?**"
If they are busy—just thank them and be glad that your resume is on the top.

Typical interview questions

- **Tell me about the work that you performed with your previous company?**
  Try to match your previous skills with skills needed in this position.

- **What did you like about working there?**
  Once again try to make the connection, if possible from your old job to the new job.
  For example: *A route sales driver applying for a customer service position;*
  I like serving the customers.

- **Why did you leave your last job?**
  The job was no longer appropriate, as it involved too much lifting/typing /standing.
  I wanted more opportunity for advancement.

- **Tell me about your other jobs?**
  Talk about related skills.

- **Why is there a gap in your employment?**
  I needed some time off, but I am ready to go back to work.

- **What was your most challenging task at your previous employment?**
  Pick something related to the new job, talk about how you overcame this obstacle.

Typical interview questions

- **What are your major strengths?**
  Use those strength words!

- **What are your major weaknesses?**
  You can also use your strength words, try to match your weaknesses with the job; for example, *I tend to be too meticulous or sometimes I'm too independent.*

- **What hours can you work?**
  Be honest but flexible!

- **What do you like to do in your spare time?**
  Mention your hobbies.

- **Are you able to perform the essential functions of the position with or without reasonable accommodations?**
  If you can do the job—even if you need accomodations—say YES.

- **How do you think that you would like working here?**
  Show you are motivated by being enthusiastic.

Different types of follow-up.

Thank you note or card, keep it simple.

Example:

Dear _________________,
Thank you for taking the time to interview me last (Day of week) for the position of ______________.

I enjoyed meeting you and learning about your company. I look forward to talking with you again soon regarding the opportunity of working for your company.

Sincerely,

Telephone call follow-up.

Example:

Hello, Is (name of the person you had the interview with) there? This is (your name), I interviewed with you last (day of week) and I am calling to follow up, to determine if you had a chance to make a decision regarding the position of __________________?
Am I catching you at a bad time?

In Person.

Example:

Not necessarily the best type of follow-up, unless it is convenient. It is mostly appropriate if you have some additional information, such as a letter of reference or sample to drop off which might have an impact on being hired.
Go on a time when they would generally not be busy. It is not appropriate to drop in during their rush hour. Do not stay too long.

After the interview

Follow-up lets the employer know that you are interested in the job and that you want the opportunity to work for them.
An average of six contacts with an employer is necessary to be hired for the job. Any initial contact, interview, and follow-up counts.

Don't give up until you have a definite negative six.

	1st contact	2nd contact
Employer or contact person		
Date		
Type of follow-up		
Comments:		

	3rd contact	4th contact
Employer or contact person		
Date		
Type of follow-up		
Comments		

	5th contact	6th contact
Employer or contact person		
Date		
Type of follow-up		
Comments		

Referrals
1.
2.
3.

Psychological pre-employment testing

This is legal. These are some of the questions that you may be asked. They are generally multiple choice and you are asked to choose the best answer.

- What would you do if you saw a co-worker stealing?
- What would you do if you saw a customer stealing?
- How would you handle a situation where a co-worker was threatening you?
- What would you do if a customer/employee/supervisor asked you to do something against company policy/protocol?
- How would you handle thefts or threats by/from a supervisor?
- How would you handle a screaming insistent customer/employee/supervisor?
- How would you handle/react to sexual advances from customer/employee/supervisor?
- What would you do as an employee when all assigned work has been completed? Go home? Sweep the floor? Clean up? Put your feet up and wait? Ask for more work? Get on the phone?
- How would you respond to a supervisor from a different department asking you to do something outside your normal job requirement?

How do you answer these questions?

Employers look for honest employees that do not steal.

They also look for employee that work hard.

Generally, employers want you to talk to your immediate supervisor, first, if there are any problems on the job.

Doing anything which goes against company policy is not acceptable.

I am worried that the medications I take will show up when I go in for drug testing. If they find out about the medications I use, I will never get the job.

You can **stop worrying** if the employer uses a testing laboratory and a Medical Review Officer (MRO) service to handle the drug testing. If your test results are positive the results will be sent to the Medical Review Officer who will call you for an explanation. That is your opportunity to explain the legally prescribed medications. The MRO will then report the test as a negative to the employer. ** **The employer will not be informed of your legal meds. ****

However, **if drug testing is performed at their place of business,** at a small doctor's office, or if the employer does not use a testing laboratory **it is possible that the employer will find out** about the prescription drugs. The employer may or may not give you a chance to explain your medication use. Some will be thoughtful and try to accommodate your needs while others will not.

Regardless of the situation, be truthful when asked. Above all**, know your limitations and the effect of medications on your ability to safety and properly perform the job for which you are applying.** Some employers have a Safety Policy that requires employees to report prescription medications that can cause a safety risk.

The use of illegal drugs or abuse of legal substances is not protected under the ADA. Drug testing typically screens for narcotics, cocaine, stimulants, marijuana, alcohol, and some prescription medications. **An employer will probably not hire you if illegal drugs are found in your urine.**

An employer may not discriminate in hiring you unless the medications you take make it unsafe for you to perform the job.

It is illegal for a testing laboratory **to release any medical information** to current or prospective employers **except to report the presence of illegal drugs or a safety risk.**

A doctor can disqualify you for the job **if the medications you take would interfere with the job for which you are applying.**

For example: A truck driver who takes narcotics for pain would not meet safety regulations. Other safety sensitive jobs include aircraft operations and operating commercial boats. These jobs are strictly regulated by the Department of Transportation (DOT) , Federal Aviation Administration (FAA) and the U.S. Coast Guard.

Preparing for the Interview

Check all that apply.

- ❑ **Special grooming - polished shoes, hair styled, nails appropriate length**
- ❑ **Clean, work/interview appropriate No open toes**
- ❑ **Completed practice application with names and dates of previous employment, references, and schools.**
- ❑ **Two forms of identification**
- ❑ **Name of person who will be interviewing you**
- ❑ **Date and time of interview**
- ❑ **Knowledge of possible reasonable accommodations**

After the interview

How did you do?

- ❑ Arrived on time for the interview
- ❑ Brought a pen, examples of your work, and extra copy of your resume
- ❑ Presented skills and abilities in positive fashion
- ❑ Smiled
- ❑ Refrained from ‘bad-mouthing’ previous employers
- ❑ Shared relevant information with prospective employer
- ❑ Answered interviewer questions appropriately—sticking to question and not giving out too much unrelated information
- ❑ Asked appropriate questions about job duties and their expectations
- ❑ Showed enthusiasm
- ❑ Utilized appropriate body language-shaking hands, making good eye contact
- ❑ Did not try to extend interview when interviewer gave signs that it was over.
- ❑ Thanked employer for interview
- ❑ Set a time frame to find out whether you have been hired for the job
- ❑ Got the name of the interviewer
- ❑ Increased your knowledge of the company, its philosophies, work hours, benefits and job responsibilities

Coping with Job Search Stress

Rejection is common during a job search and can affect your self-esteem. Taking extra care of yourself will help you to cope with this additional stress.

Include a least one positive activity per day

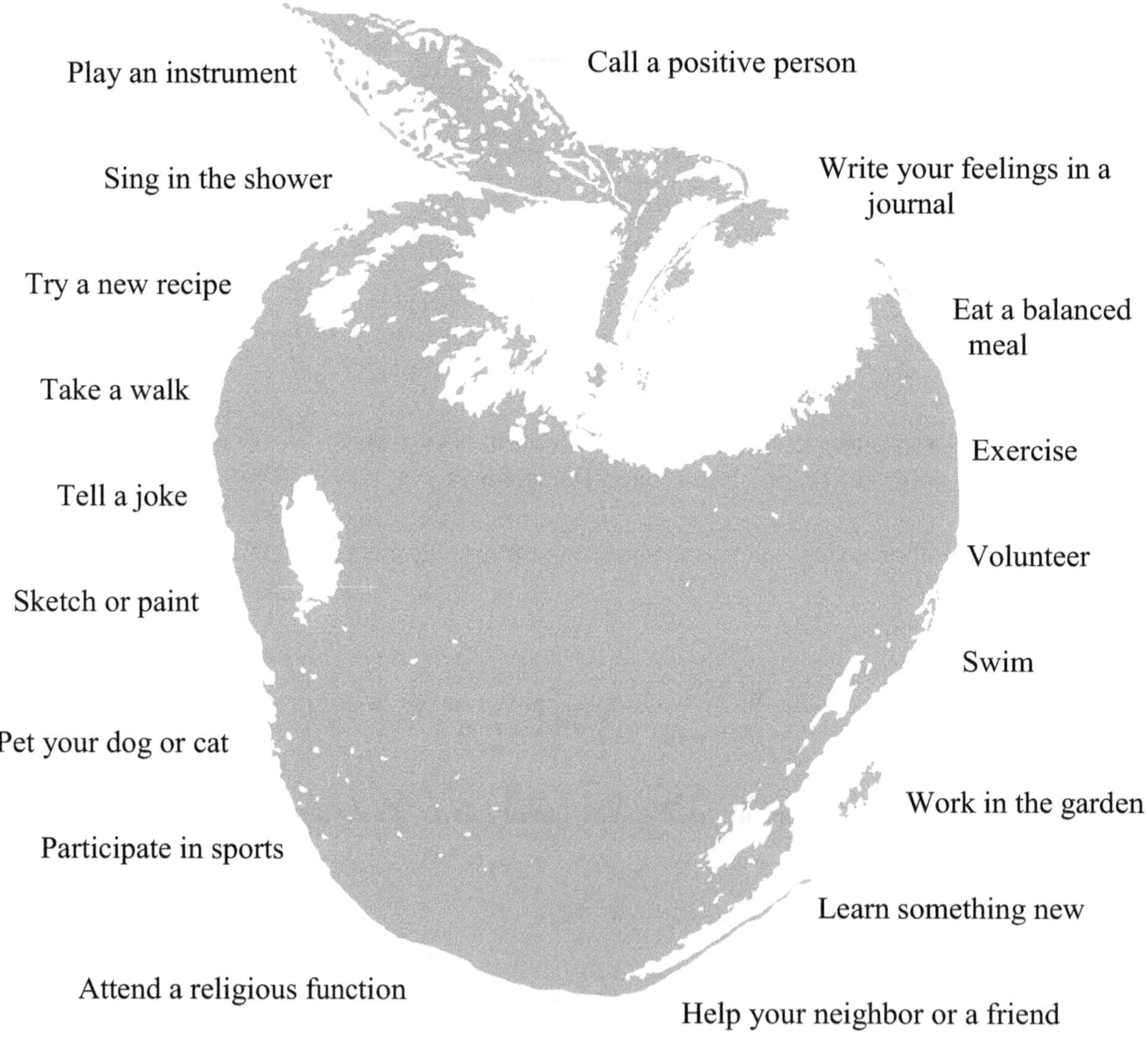

You can manage your feelings.

Try saying or thinking three positives things for every negative thought about yourself or others.

You got the job, congratulations !!!

How are you feeling?

- ❑ **Happy**
- ❑ **Scared**
- ❑ **Excited**
- ❑ **Anxious**
- ❑ **Fearful**
- ❑ **Relieved**

All of these feelings are normal after being offered a job. People are generally happy to find a job, yet scared they might not know how to do the job or worried that they will not fit in.

Training is a normal part of any new hire. It is expected that you will need to learn the procedures at your new place of work.

It is possible that "you will not fit in" at first. It takes a little time to build workplace relationships, but the employer thinks you will fit in just fine. That's why the company hired YOU !

You are going to start work, what's next?

- ❑ **Do I have my uniform/work clothes ready?**
- ❑ **Are child care arrangements in place?**
- ❑ **Do I know how to get to work?**
- ❑ **How long does it take to get to work?**
- ❑ **Can I make it on time? What about a trial run?**
- ❑ **Do I need reasonable accommodations? If so, what?**
- ❑ **Have I contacted my support systems to let them know the good news and to allow them to continue to support me through this transition?**
- ❑ **Smile! You have successfully completed your job search and are ready to go to work now!**

Your first day at work.

Well, pretty exciting, wasn't it?

Lots of new people, new ideas, machines, and so much to do and learn.

Are you a little tired? Nervous?

Wondering how you did?

Check all that apply.

- ❑ **I got to work on time.**
- ❑ **My children were picked up on time.**
- ❑ **I was able to get along with my co-workers.**
- ❑ **I met some interesting people.**
- ❑ **I learned something new.**
- ❑ **I earned some money.**
- ❑ **I was able to be helpful.**
- ❑ **I was productive.**

Relax, enjoy - It will get easier and less confusing.

You will get to know your co-workers and build relationships.

You are beginning a new phase of your life!

ISBN -13: 978-097152220-6

Humans are not all made alike. Each person has their own special qualities.

One person may be very athletic and have strong legs and arms, but have a slow mind.

Another person might be creative and have strong beliefs and values, but have no feet to stand on.

The nice thing about being a unique individual is that different jobs require different abilities.

Other books by PAULA REUBEN VIEILLET, MA, CVE

Instructor's Guide: Disabilities /Different Abilities:
A New Perspective for Job Hunters

Great resource for counselor training, job clubs, individual assessment and case management. Step-by-step instructions facilitate the use of the client workbook with groups and individuals.

www.MyEmploymentOptions.com

Contact: Paula Vieillet, MA, CVE (800) 441-3114

About the Author

Paula Reuben Vieillet is the president of Employment Options, Inc., a National provider of vocational rehabilitation services and a certified Employment Network in the Social Security Ticket to Work program.

She has earned a Master's Degree in Adult Education: Training and Development, and is a Nationally Certified Vocational Evaluator and Licensed Rehabilitation Counselor. She has worked in the field since 1987.

Her three-step job search strategy designed to increase self-esteem and self-advocacy has helped many people who have previously been unable to secure employment, find suitable and satisfying work within a very short period of time through proper assessment and advanced job placement techniques. Employment Option's job placement statistics are exceptional with even the most challenging populations.

www.ingramcontent.com/pod-product-compliance
Lightning Source LLC
LaVergne TN
LVHW061252100826
845148LV00008B/1104
* 9 7 8 0 9 7 1 5 2 2 2 0 6 *